ANCIENT WORLDS

ANCIENT RULERS WHO WRECKED THE WORLD

Martin Gitlin

45TH PARALLEL PRESS

Published in the United States of America by Cherry Lake Publishing Group
Ann Arbor, Michigan
www.cherrylakepublishing.com

Reading Adviser: Beth Walker Gambro, MS, Ed., Reading Consultant, Yorkville, IL

Photo Credits: © Lambros Kazan /Shutterstock, cover, title page; © Nastasic/iStock.com, 4; © Kizel Cotiw-an/Shutterstock, 7; © DaLiu/Shutterstock, 8; © Old Books Images/Alamy Stock Photo, 11; © Alireza Hosseinzadeh/Shutterstock, 12; © TasfotoNL/Shutterstock, 14; © Sergey Kohl/Shutterstock, 16; Internet Archive Book Images, No restrictions, via Wikimedia Commons, 18; © Album/Alamy Stock Photo, 20; Getty Villa (No restrictions or Copyrighted fre e use), via Wikimedia Commons, 23; © Nastasic/iStock.com, 24; © Grafissimo/iStock.com, 26; Unknown source, Public domain, via Wikimedia Commons, 28; © rootstock/Shutterstock, 30

Graphic Element Credits: Graphic Element Credits: Cover, multiple interior pages: © Andrey_Kuzmin/Shutterstock, © cajoer/Shutterstock, © GUSAK OLENA/Shutterstock, © Eky Studio/Shutterstock

45TH Parallel Press is an imprint of Cherry Lake Publishing Group.

Library of Congress Cataloging-in-Publication Data has been filed and is available at catalog.loc.gov.

Cherry Lake Publishing Group would like to acknowledge the work of the Partnership for 21st Century Learning, a Network of Battelle for Kids. Please visit http://www.battelleforkids.org/networks/p21 for more information.

Printed in the United States of America

Note from publisher: Websites change regularly, and their future contents are outside of our control. Supervise children when conducting any recommended online searches for extended learning opportunities.

About the Author
Martin Gitlin is an educational book author based in Connecticut. He won more than 45 awards as a newspaper journalist from 1991 to 2002. Included was a first-place award from the Associated Press. That organization voted him as one of the top four feature writers in Ohio in 2002. Martin has had about 250 books published since 2006. Most of them were written for students. He has authored many books about history.

TABLE OF CONTENTS

Introduction...4

Chapter 1: The Murderous Madman.........................8

Chapter 2: The Brutal Beast of Persia..................12

Chapter 3: The Ruthless Ruler...............................16

Chapter 4: The Revolting Roman............................20

Chapter 5: The Horrible Hun..................................24

Chapter 6: The Wild Killer.....................................28

Glossary...32

Learn More..32

Index...32

INTRODUCTION

Cambyses II became King of the Achaemenid Empire in 530 BCE.

World history had many bad rulers. These rulers wanted power. They wanted land. They wanted riches. They killed their enemies. They even killed friends. They wanted loyal people. They used fear to control others. They punished disloyal people.

Ancient times were marked by war. Some rulers went too far. They destroyed all who tried to stop them. They wished to take over other nations. They created armies. They sent soldiers into battle. They started wars. Millions were killed.

These rulers were bad. But they became famous. Their names live in **infamy**. Infamy means gaining fame by being brutal. They're known because of their evil deeds. This is not a good thing.

Morality is knowing right from wrong. It keeps changing. What was moral in the past might not be moral today. Rulers today struggle with it. Times change. Ideas change. People have to change how they think.

Violence was more accepted in ancient times. It was considered fair punishment. Some rulers were violent. Some even liked to murder. Some liked to torture victims. They ordered it to stay in power. They did it to keep people fearful.

Wars have changed the world. Rulers today can be evil. But ancient leaders could be **tyrants**. Tyrants are brutal leaders. They hold all the power. Some tyrants were worse than others.

Caligula was a Roman **emperor** from 37 CE to 41 CE. An emperor is a ruler of an empire. It is said he made senators fight in the Colosseum's arena.

CHAPTER ONE

Phalaris was brutal. He built a temple. He armed his workers. He seized power.

The Murderous Madman

Death was a common punishment in ancient times. But one tyrant went beyond this. He tortured his victims. His name was Phalaris. He ruled in the 5th century BCE. He was a **despot**. He ruled Acragas, now Agrigento. This is a city on an island. It's off the coast of Italy. Today, the island is called Sicily.

Phalaris did some good things. He built a temple. He supplied water. He built strong buildings. He made the walls stronger. He protected the city. He increased trade. He hosted sporting events.

But he was not kind. It was dangerous to upset him. Phalaris tortured his enemies. Myth says he had a bronze bull statue. He forced victims inside. A fire was started underneath. Anyone inside the bull was roasted alive. Screams of pain were heard.

His first victim was Perillus. Perillus was a **sculptor**. Sculptors create art. They make models. They make structures. Perillus made the bronze bull. Phalaris used him to test it. The bronze bull worked. Perillus was burned to death.

Phalaris was mean. But he received justice. His enemies turned on him. They burned him in his own bull. He was killed the same way as his victims.

Some in Sicily liked Phalaris. They agreed with what he did. They thought the bronze bull was a good punishment. But history tells a different story. Phalaris is seen today as a murderous madman.

Phalaris was known for his bronze bull. In the end, he was also its victim.

CHAPTER TWO

This is the tomb of Cyrus the Great. He is a hero to many people. His son, Cambyses II, was a cruel king.

The Brutal Beast of Persia

Cambyses II was a king. He ruled the Achaemenid Empire. This empire existed from 550 to 330 BCE. It was called Persia. That country is now Iran. His father was Cyrus the Great. Cyrus passed the throne to his son. That was a bad idea. Cambyses was hungry for power. He governed ruthlessly. His armies attacked Egypt. They invaded Africa.

Cambyses was also mean. He proved it after taking over Egypt. Amasis ruled Egypt. He did this about 6 months earlier. He had died. Cambyses destroyed the **corpse** of Amasis. He stabbed it. He tore the hair out. He burned it.

That was only one awful story. Herodotus was a Greek author. He told other stories. He wrote that Cambyses killed the Apis bull. That was a sacred animal in Egypt. Herodotus said Cambyses stabbed it with a sword.

The Apis bull died from its wounds. People worshiped the Apis bull. Priests searched for another one. Egyptians celebrated when one was found. But they were mad at Cambyses.

Herodotus had more stories. Cambyses may have killed Smerdis. Smerdis was his brother. Cambyses may have married his sister. Then he killed her. Herodotus said Cambyses killed many others. Among them was the son of a nobleman. Cambyses buried 12 Persian noblemen alive. He taunted statues of Egyptian gods.

Are these stories true? No one knows for sure. Much of Herodotus's writings have been disproved. But was Cambyses really cruel? Yes, he was.

Herodotus was a Greek historian. He was also a geographer.

A NICE STORY

Some ancient rulers started wars. They were known for cruelty. They killed people. But others had kind hearts. Among them was Vespasian.

Vespasian was an emperor. He ruled the Roman Empire. He did this from 69 to 79 CE. He was known for being smart. He understood his citizens. He helped victims of natural disasters.

He was also generous toward writers and teachers. He paid them for their work.

Most Romans loved Vespasian. Some showed dislike. But Vespasian respected everyone. That included those who didn't like him.

Vespasian helped those he ruled. He improved the city. He spent money on the Temple of Peace. He also helped build public baths. The Colosseum is a stadium. It was built during his rule.

CHAPTER THREE

Nero had his rivals killed. This allowed him to take power.

The Ruthless Ruler

Nero took over the Roman Empire. He did this at age 16. He did this in 54 CE. He ruled for nearly 15 years. He was brutal.

Nero may have killed his mother. His mother was Agrippina the Younger. First, he tried to poison her. Then he tried other things. He tried to drown her in a sinking boat. He tried to crush her by a falling ceiling. Some stories say he **framed** her. Frame means to set someone up. He said she was trying to kill him. He then staged her death. He made it look like she killed herself.

Another story says Nero was to marry Claudia Octavio. He was 11 years old. Claudia was his stepsister. Nero and Claudia finally wed. He was 15 years old. Nine years later, he divorced her. But that was not enough. He slit her wrists. Then he had her **suffocated** in a steam bath. Suffocate means to stop one from breathing. Her head was cut off. It was brought to him. Many people don't believe this story is true.

No woman wanted to marry Nero! His 2nd wife also died. Her name was Poppaea Sabina.

The city of Rome caught fire. This happened in 64 CE. The fire lasted a week. It destroyed most of Rome. One famous story states Nero "**fiddled** while Rome burned." A fiddle is another name for a violin. Some people think Nero set the city on fire. They think he did this to build a new city.

The story about the fiddle is untrue. The fiddle didn't exist at that time. The story just shows how Nero didn't care about people.

Nero is known by all as a madman. Rome burned under his rule.

MYSTERY SOLVED OR UNSOLVED?

Harmodius and Aristogeiton were Greeks. They weren't special. They weren't leaders. They weren't artists. But they became legends. This happened in the 6th century BCE. They killed Hipparchus. Hipparchus ruled Athens.

Little is known about Harmodius and Aristogeiton. Thucydides was an author. He wrote about them. He said Harmodius and Aristogeiton were lovers.

Hipparchus ruled Athens. He did this with brother. His brother was Hippias.

But why was Hipparchus killed? Nobody knows for sure. One idea is that Hipparchus loved Harmodius. Harmodius rejected him. Aristogeiton got mad. So Hipparchus got mad too. He shamed Harmodius's sister. He did this at a public event.

Harmodius was upset. He wanted to kill Hipparchus and Hippias. So did Aristogeiton. They plotted his death. They hired killers. They all hid knives. They stabbed Hipparchus to death. But Hippias escaped.

CHAPTER FOUR

Commodus's life inspired a movie. It was called *Gladiator*. It was made in the year 2000.

The Revolting Roman

Lucius Adurelius Commodus was a Roman ruler. He was nasty. He has been compared to Nero.

His father was Marcus Aurelius. Aurelius was a Roman emperor. He was a wonderful ruler. But his son was the opposite.

Commodus killed many Romans. He punished his enemies. He did mean things.

He was born in 161 CE. He had many brothers. His brothers all died by the time he was 8 years old. He was the only heir. He helped run the Roman Empire. He did this at age 15.

He became crueler with age. He married Bruttia Crispina. He did this at age 16. He later had her killed. He thought she was going to kill him.

Some think Commodus killed for money. He did need a lot. He paid for huge **gladiator** games. Gladiators are warriors. Some fought to the death. They did this for sport. Commodus bought expensive animals. The animals fought the gladiators.

Commodus had a huge ego. He thought he was Hercules. Hercules was a **demigod**. This means half-human, half-god. Commodus wanted statues of himself. He chopped off the head of one statue. Then he replaced it. He added a head that looked more like him. He also tried to rename Rome. He wanted to call it "Colony of Commodus." This was to honor himself.

Narcissus worked for him. Senators hired Narcissus. They hired him to kill Commodus. The plot was a success. Narcissus killed him in 192 CE.

Commodus was Emperor of Rome from 177 CE to 192 CE.

CHAPTER FIVE

Attila broke a peace treaty with Rome. He attacked Roman cities.

The Horrible Hun

Attila the Hun may have been born in Pannonia. That is in modern-day Hungary. It was part of the Roman Empire during the 400s CE. Attila was among the cruelest rulers ever.

Priscus was an ancient writer. He said Attila was quiet. Attila didn't have a bad temper. But he had wild eyes. That scared people.

Attila showed his wickedness. He took over the Hunnic Empire. He ruled it with Bleda. Bleda was his brother. They did this in 434 CE. Attila feared Bleda wanted to reign alone. He felt threatened. So he killed him.

The Huns were brutal under Attila. They would **impale** or **crucify** their victims. Impale is to pierce with something sharp. Crucify is to hang on a cross.

Attila loved power. He invaded Western Europe. He did this in 451 CE. Some think his army had 200,000 men. His soldiers wiped out all in their path. They wrecked villages. They wrecked churches. They wrecked markets. They wrecked farms. They killed everyone along the way.

Attila expanded his empire. It reached modern-day Germany, Russia, and Ukraine. He caused over 40 million deaths. He died in 453 CE. Some think he ordered those who buried him to be killed. He wanted his burial site kept secret.

Attila the Hun at the Battle of Catalaunian Plains (450 CE)

ANCIENT RULES

How did Roman emperors seize power? How did they maintain it? Some used force. They killed their enemies. Or they went to war. They conquered other nations. That expanded their empires.

They required approval by the Roman Senate. The Senate governed the city. They had a lot of power.

Emperors did many things to stay on top. One was earning support of the army. Others were sons of emperors. They had been handed power.

Senators could end an emperor's rule. They did this by vote. The Roman army also had power. It could cause an emperor to be overthrown.

Even the people played a role. They protested against tyrants. The Senate and army wanted to keep Romans happy. Unpopular emperors didn't last long.

CHAPTER SIX

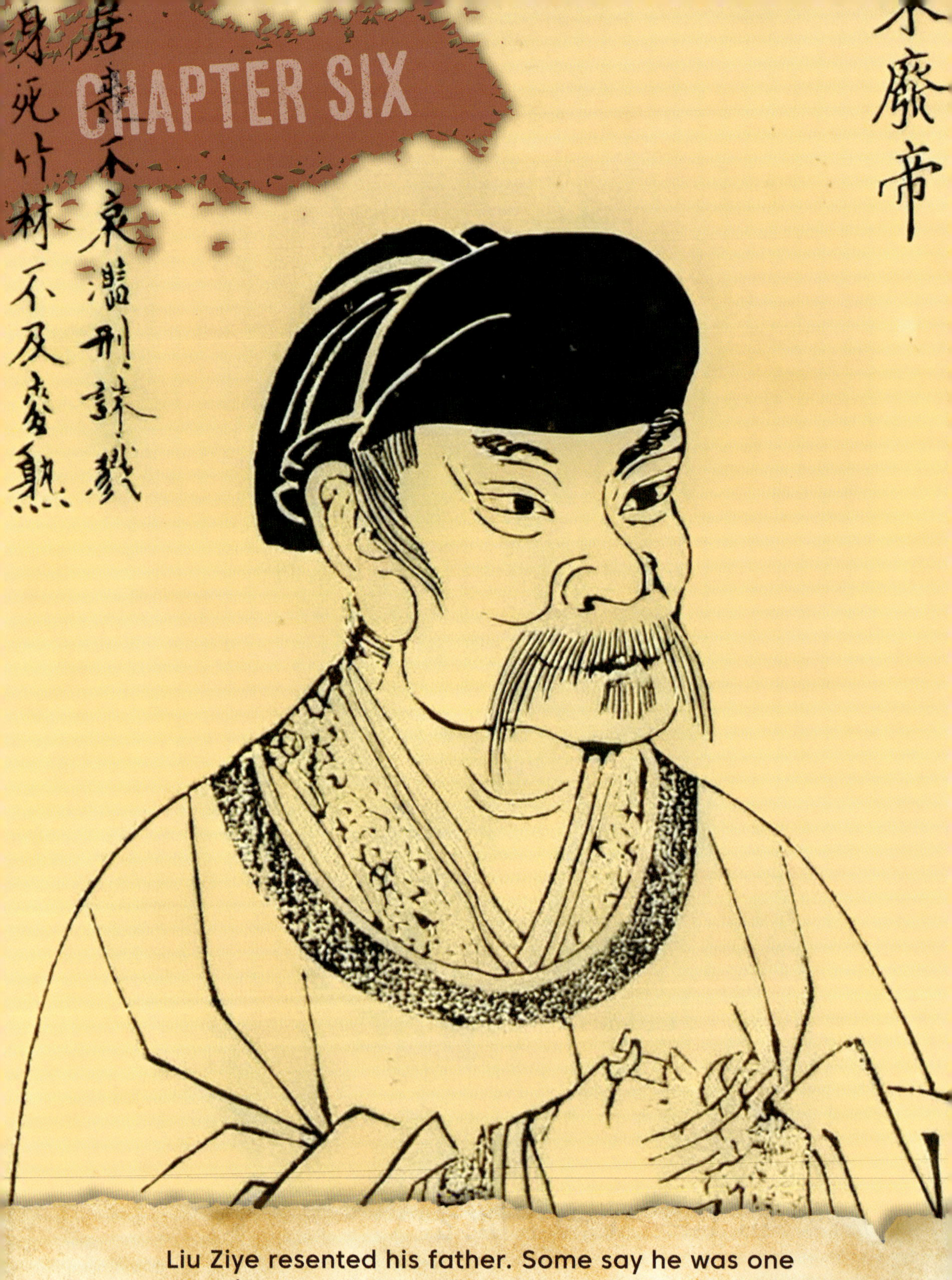

Liu Ziye resented his father. Some say he was one of Liu's greatest enemies.

The Wild Killer

Liu Ziye had a lot of power. He ruled the Liu Song **dynasty**. Dynasty means ruling family. Liu went on a murder **spree** in 464 CE. Spree means a short period of doing something.

He died in 465 CE or 466 CE. One of his enemies made sure of that.

Some think that among his enemies was his father. His father was Emperor Xiaowu. Xiaowu wanted Liu's younger brother to take the throne. One rumor says Liu forced his brother to kill himself.

Xiaowu died. With his brother dead, Liu inherited the throne at only 15 years old. Then he took the name Emperor Qianfei. He would not have made his father proud. It was said he was a bad ruler. He acted without thinking. Worst of all, he killed many people. He killed government officials. He killed his own family members.

Qianfei killed all those who worked with Xiaowu. He arrested his uncles. He feared they'd revolt. His personal life was also disturbing. It was filled with abuse.

Qianfei lasted 1 year as emperor. Shou Jizhi worked for him. He killed him. This happened in 465 CE or 466 CE.

Many were likely relieved when Emperor Qianfei was killed.

VERY IMPORTANT PEOPLE

Who's the most famous woman in ancient history? It might be Cleopatra. She was queen of Egypt. She was a lover of Julius Caesar. She later married Mark Antony. Both were Roman military leaders. Egypt fell under Roman rule.

Cleopatra was born around 69 BCE. Her father was an Egyptian ruler. She lived a rich life. Cleopatra became queen. She did this before the age of 20.

Cleopatra soon made friends with Caesar. That helped her maintain her rule. She invited him on a trip. They traveled up the Nile River. Cleopatra later gave birth to their son. That caused a scandal in Rome. Caesar was already married. But he stayed with Cleopatra. Caesar was killed in 44 BCE.

The murder alarmed Cleopatra. She was in danger. Caesar had placed a gold statue of her in a nearby temple. She had insisted on being called "queen." Cleopatra was hated in Rome. She married Mark Antony. They lost a war. She killed herself in 30 BCE. It's said she let a deadly snake bite her.

GLOSSARY

corpse (KORPS) a dead body

crucify (KROO-suh-fie) to kill a person by nailing or binding their body to a cross

demigod (DEH-mee-gawd) a mythological being who is part human and part god

despot (DEH-sput) a cruel, powerful ruler

dynasties (DIYE-nuh-steez) ruling families

emperor (EM-puhr-uhr) the ruler of an empire

fiddled (FIH-duhld) played the violin

framed (FRAYMD) set up for a crime

gladiator (GLA-dee-ay-tur) an ancient Roman who fought animals and other men

impale (im-PAYL) to run a sharp object completely through someone's body

infamy (IN-fuh-mee) evil or shameful reputation

morality (muh-RA-luh-tee) inner beliefs of what is right or wrong

sculptor (SKULP-tur) an artist who creates by carving or molding

spree (SPREE) a short period of doing something

suffocated (SUH-fuh-kayt-id) died because of lack of air

tyrants (TIYE-ruhnts) rulers who abuse their power by treating their subjects harshly

LEARN MORE

Fet, Catherine. *Ancient Rome for Kids Through the Lives of its Heroes, Emperors, and Philosophers*. Independently Published, 2020.

Pipe, Jim. *You Wouldn't Want to Be Cleopatra*. New York: Franklin Watts, 2017.

Search online with an adult:
Ducksters: Ancient Egypt for Kids.

INDEX

Achaemenid Empire, 4, 13
armies, 5, 13, 26, 27
Attila the Hun, 24–26

Caesar, Julius, 31
Caligula, 7
Cambyses II, 4, 12–14
China, 28–30
Cleopatra, 31
Commodus, Lucius Aurelius, 20–23
conquests, 5, 13, 26, 27
Cyrus the Great, 12–13

Egypt, 13–14, 31
emperors, 7, 15, 16–18, 20–23, 27, 28–30

fear, use of, 5–6, 25

gladiators, 20, 22
good works, 9, 15
Greece, 13, 14, 19

Herodotus, 13–14
historical accounts, 13–14, 19, 25
Hunnic Empire, 25–26

killing enemies, 5, 9, 15, 16, 26, 27, 30
killing family and friends, 5, 14, 17–18, 19, 22, 25, 26, 29–30

legends, 14, 18, 19, 26
Liu Ziye (Emperor Qianfei), 28–30

modern rulers, 6
money, 5, 22

Nero, 16–18, 21

Phalaris, 8–11
power, 5–6, 8, 13, 16, 26, 27, 29, 30
punishment, 5–6, 9–10, 21

Roman senators, 7, 27
Rome, 7, 15, 16–18, 21–23, 24, 27, 31
rulers killed, 10–11, 19, 22, 30, 31

suicide, 17, 29, 31

Thucydides, 19
torture, 6, 9–11, 14, 25

Vespasian, 15

wars, 5–6, 15, 27